the *bare-bones guide* to . . .

GENEALOGY

Researching and Recording Your Family History

by
Mary T. McGlone

pilot books

Copyright © 1997, 1998 by
PILOT BOOKS
127 Sterling Avenue
Greenport, NY 11944

Library of Congress Catalog Card Number: 97-30026

Library of Congress Cataloging in Publication Data

McGlone, Mary T., 1961-
the bare-bones guide to . . . Genealogy Researching and
Recording your family history / by Mary T. McGlone
        p. cm.
    Includes bibliographical references and index.
    ISBN 0-87576-213-1 (alk. paper)
      1. United States—Genealogy—Manuals, handbooks,
etc. I. Title.
CS47.M338   1997
929'.1'072073—dc21   97-30026
                                  CIP

For my grandmothers,
Milada Hedbavny
and
Agnes Farrell

About the author

Mary McGlone grew up in Mamaroneck, New York, received her B.A. in English from Iona College and M.A. from the University of Iowa. In addition to writing for a variety of publications, she has taught high school English and college writing courses.

Genealogy has always fascinated Ms. McGlone, who recently documented her own family history, giving her the perfect head start on researching and writing this book. She currently lives on the North Fork of Long Island, where she balances writing projects with environmental activities.

Table of Contents

How many people have been born, lived rich, loving lives, laughed and wept, been part of creation, and are now forgotten, unremembered by anybody walking the earth today?

—*Madeleine L'Engle*

To the Reader:

There is a tinted photograph of my great-great-grandmother hanging above my bookcase, a gift from my grandmother shortly before she died. It shows a calm, strong-looking woman with clear eyes and I find myself looking at it frequently, fascinated by the connection between us.

We all have a family history that intrigues and somehow defines us, yet most of us know very little beyond our ethnic background, perhaps our grandparents' full names. Unless we seek and record the facts of our heritage, they are likely to slip away forever.

Whether you want only a bit of information — a glimpse of your family's past — or plan to do an extensive genealogy and family history as a gift to your family, this book will guide you in your search for information and show you how to organize your materials as you proceed. It will help you finish your project, no matter how large or small.

In this fast-paced world, knowledge of our ancestry can ground us. Uncovering our family's history is a concrete way of honoring their struggles, their joys, their passions, their faith. This book is for those of you who want to know more stories behind the lives that came before us, stories that can lead us into ourselves.

Getting Started

Chapter 1

Before You Begin

There is more than one way to go about this project; how you choose to proceed has as much to do with your personality as the material at your disposal. Each chapter of this book focuses on a different aspect of a genealogical search and recording. The first 11 chapters are about gathering and organizing information; the last three offer ways to share this information.

While we suggest that you read the entire book for important background information, each chapter is relatively independent, so you *can* skip those that do not pertain to your project or proceed in any order that suits you. For instance, if your main priority is to organize an album of old photographs, you might begin with Chapter 12.

Whether you enjoy working on a computer and accessing information through the Internet or prefer the solidity of correspondence, you will find different strategies throughout the book so you can use the one that most appeals to you.

A few hints before you begin:

- *Remember your enthusiasm for the project and keep your goals in sight.*

You are about to undertake an admirable, exciting, sometimes daunting task. The most essential resources you bring to it are your enthusiasm, perseverance and determination. You will have many satisfying moments; savor them. File them away to inspire you during long days of searching for information. Keep the value of what you are doing in mind. Think of future generations and remember how much it would have meant to you if someone else had done what you are about to do.

• *Let family members know about your project.*

Draw upon their encouragement and let them help you if they offer. They can be one of the most important resources to draw upon for information and emotional sustenance.

• *Be careful.*

Keep meticulous records, write everything down. Follow up when you say you will. Verify information. Proceed in a logical, organized way (we'll show you how) so you won't waste time researching the wrong ancestor, for example. Your careful records will also be invaluable to any family member who wants to become involved or to pick up where you left off.

• *Be persistent.*

Valuable information does not come easily or quickly (though access to many records via computer makes it much faster than in the past). You will undoubtedly face some hurdles and frustrations, but remember that the only way past these rough spots is to keep going. Change direction or strategy if you need to, but keep going.

One final thought: it is generally advisable to do as much of your own research as possible and to consult a professional only if you are mired in a particular problem. There are, however, many reputable genealogists. If interested, check with a respected librarian for a referral, or browse in genealogical publications (see Appendix A) for advertisements.

Chapter 2
Using Charts

There are three basic charts that you will need to compile a family history, and several formats of each: the Ancestry Chart, the Family Information Sheet, and the Individual Information Sheet. The basis of your genealogical files, these three forms bind all your information and research together.

Ancestry Charts

Five-Generation Ancestry Chart

The most common form of the Ancestry Chart is the five-generation form (see page 6). On this chart you will record basic information (names, birth dates and places, marriage dates and places, death dates and places) about your family back to your great-great-grandparents. Visually, it gives a good overview of the information you have and is the blueprint for all your other records. It is easily expanded by adding other ancestry charts to the last generation, allowing you to go as far back as you choose or are able to. (You will notice that this chart records only your direct ancestry line and does not include information on siblings; that information is recorded on family information sheets).

The Ancestry Chart includes an individual code number for each ancestor. This coding system is a standard, easy-to-use genealogical system. You (the genealogist) are number 1; your father is number 2, your mother number 3; your father's parents are numbers 4 (father) and 5 (mother). Your mother's

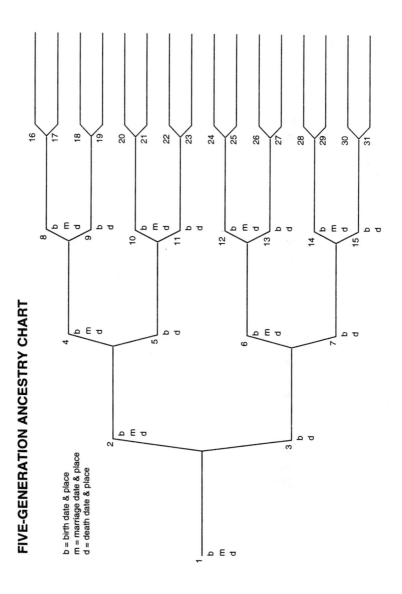

FIVE-GENERATION ANCESTRY CHART

b = birth date & place
m = marriage date & place
d = death date & place

parents are 6 (father) and 7 (mother). In this system, with the exception of the genealogist (if male), all male ancestors have even numbers and female ancestors have odd numbers. The paternal line appears visually above the maternal line.

When filling out this chart, keep a few hints in mind: *Always use complete birth names (not nicknames or married names) and include only accurate, verified information.* For instance, you may know your paternal grandmother only by her married name. In that case write only her first and middle names (if known) and leave her last (birth) name blank until you obtain that information.

First, fill out as much of this chart as you easily can. How much information you already know will help you determine your goals for research. It is better to set reasonable goals than to feel overwhelmed by trying to fill in all the unknowns in a family's history. You can always expand your project once you've met your original goals.

One common goal (much more achievable for third or fourth-generation Americans) is to trace your family's American history, going back to your ancestors' arrival in this country. Then, if time and interest allow, you may decide to explore your ancestry in other countries (see Chapter 11) which requires different strategies. It is simplest to follow one lineage at a time in your research (for example, fathers' paternal line). Since in most families the surname is carried down paternally and records were generally filed under the man's name, it will be easier to trace that line first and find information on wives within those records.

Looking at the Ancestry Chart allows you to quickly see what information you have and what you still need. As you gather information, it also helps you visualize relationships. *If you're tempted to enter information that is not yet verified, do so only if you are meticulous about identifying what you are absolutely sure of, and which information has not yet been verified.* You might want to have one chart that is "official" and proven, and another which is a draft. As you verify information, you can record it on the "official" chart. Or you can use [brackets], question marks or different color inks as ways to mark those items. Computer software programs, which utilize these charts, can be extremely helpful since information is easily added as it is discovered. Information about software programs is in Chapter 4.

Radial Ancestry Chart

An alternative to the five-generation Ancestry Chart, the Radial Ancestry Chart is used to record the same information. Notice that expanding it requires only more space on the perimeter of the semicircle; its structure is virtually endless. It can easily be made into a full circle to include your spouse's family information. While the discussions in this book are based on the assumption that you are using the standard five-generation Ancestry Chart, if you choose to use the radial format, the basic techniques remain the same and the same coding system is used.

Family Information Sheet

The second type of chart you'll need is the Family Information Sheet. Here you will record information about each family which appears on the Ancestry Chart. Be sure to identify the family by name and by ancestor's code number (for simplicity, use the man's number). For example, if you are filling in the Family Information Sheet for your mother's parents and siblings, the family chart number will be six (for her father). Each man on your ancestral chart will have a corre-

RADIAL ANCESTRY CHART

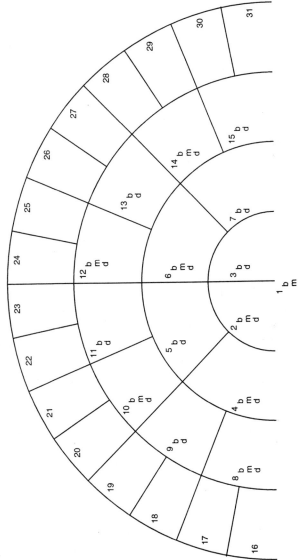

sponding Family Information Sheet (which includes his wife and children).

A sample chart is shown on page 11. There are many types of family charts available (see Appendix A, Genealogical Publishers), but all contain the following information:

- each parent's full name, birth date and place, marriage date and place, death date and place, other spouses, parents' full names

- each child's full name, birth place and date, marriage information (including spouse's name), death date and place, listed in birth order from oldest to youngest

- information on individuals' education, occupation, hobbies, or interests (optional)

Individual Information Sheet

Since these sheets contain more detailed information about each ancestor, do them after you complete as much as you can of the Ancestry and Family Charts. The Individual Information Sheets can consist simply of blank sheets of paper (always provide the full name and code number), or you can easily copy our format or other information sheets. Include standard information, such as residences, marriage(s), jobs, children, military service, and education for each individual.

To ensure accuracy and save time later, be sure to document the sources for all the information you include on each of these forms. Some sheets allow room for this. If not, it is easily done on the back; simply list the ancestor's name, information, and source.

FAMILY INFORMATION SHEET

_____ FAMILY   FAMILY CODE # _____

Birth date
Birth place   _____
Death date   Full name of husband
Burial place
Religion   _____
Education   His father
Occupation   _____
                       His mother

Birth date   _____
Birth place
Death date   Full name of wife
Burial place
Religion   _____ _____
Education   Her father
Occupation   _____
                       Her mother

Other spouses (his or hers)
                       _____
                       Marriage date

                       _____
                       Place

CHILDREN OF THIS MARRIAGE

#	Full Name	Gender	Birth (D/M/Y)	Death (D/M/Y)	Marriage (Date/To)
1					
2					
3					
4					
5					
6					
7					
8					

INDIVIDUAL INFORMATION SHEET

THE LIFE OF _____ CODE # _____
                        name of ancestor

Include information on marriage(s), children, education, military service, residences, illnesses, religious milestones, jobs, migrations, family events, deaths, etc.

YEAR	EVENT

_____ Born at _____

_____ Death. Burial place _____

Research Log

It is important to keep track of your research efforts throughout your search. This will help you avoid duplicating your efforts, allow you to double-check conflicting information, and be valuable for anyone who may continue or become involved in the genealogical research. The Research Log form below contains the basic information you will want to record.

RESEARCH LOG

Ancestor's name: _____ Code # _____

Information sought: _____

_____

Date of search: _____

Location: _____

Source (i.e., book's title, author, year, pages): _____

_____

Information found: _____

_____

_____

Comments: _____

_____

_____

_____

Even if you feel sure of the facts you record, it is important to verify the information with at least one other member of your family. Once you have filled in all you can of the Ancestry Chart (and don't be discouraged if it's not much), contact family members who might be able to help you. They will be your first resources for several reasons:

- Several relatives with reliable memories can give you a lot of accurate, firsthand information (you may even find that someone has already begun the family genealogy).

- It is much easier to confirm information than to discover it.

- Establishing contacts now will make it easy to confer with people later. As you discover interesting or conflicting information, family members are often glad to embellish on facts once they know of your interest.

- It's good to have family interest and support at the beginning of your project to spur you on and you will probably find that doing your research with the appreciation of others in mind will make the process more enjoyable.

Some people find it easiest to begin by going through old family photographs with an older relative to identify people and gather information in a conversational, relaxed manner. Others prefer beginning with the Ancestry Chart and branching off to Family Information Sheets as they proceed. There is no right or wrong way, as long as you do everything logically and carefully and gather information in an organized way.

Chapter 3

Getting Organized

A loose-leaf binder is the simplest way to keep your family history files organized and accessible throughout your project. Even if you choose to store most of your information on a computer, always keep paper back up files, records, and documents. The loose-leaf format makes organization easy (it is simple to add, remove or reorganize documents or other information) and easily holds many types of paper (letters, documents, charts, notes).

In addition, you'll probably need a miscellaneous file for documents that are too bulky, delicate, or detailed to include in your binder. This can be a box or file drawer that holds individual files within it. Depending on how you choose to organize your material, you may file these papers by place name, family name, or individual code number (more on this later).

To get started, you will need a few simple supplies:

- a loose-leaf binder, with a large capacity (1 1/2" - 2" ring)
- copies of charts
- dividers
- Rolodex or index file box and cards to keep track of contacts
- miscellaneous file

Really, that's all that's essential. Depending on the process you use and how extensive your project becomes, there are other supplies you may find helpful. For example, you might consider a genealogy computer program (see Chapter 4), and you will need archival photographic supplies if you intend to work with photographs (see Chapter 12). But the basics of organizing information are that simple. Suggestion: splurge on little "perks", like good quality paper, colored pens, whatever helps you stay excited about this project.

Organizing the Binder

In the binder:

- Ancestry Chart
- Family Information Sheets
- Individual Information Sheets
- Dividers labeled with relevant surnames or family code numbers
- Supporting documents (copies)
- Research Log

Optional:

- U.S. map to chart family migrations
- Map(s) of relevant countries of origin
- An alphabetical list of surnames with corresponding code numbers

Here are two simple ways to organize your files; your choice is primarily whether you prefer working with names or numbers:

- Divide the binder into sections by family name. In each section include those forms which pertain to that name. It is advisable to arrange forms in order from most general (Ancestry Chart) to most specific (Individual Sheets) for ease in filing. This system (and the one below) allows you to add sections easily.

- Another commonly used system is to file everything in the binder numerically, using the individual code numbers (in this system, the family information sheets will be even numbers only). You can file the individual sheets behind the relevant family sheet, or have a separate section for them.

You can also use the binder to hold copies of documents and photographs (*because they are frequently fragile, it is best to make copies and keep the originals in a safer place*), an alphabetical list of ancestors, and a map to chart your family's migrations. As your files grow, reference materials such as these will prove very helpful.

Miscellaneous File

As stated earlier, regardless of how you organize your binder, you will need a filing system for various documents that it is impractical to put in the binder. This can be a box or file drawer. Before filing, label everything with the corresponding code number. Within the file you can organize documents in file folders by family name or number or by document type (birth and death records, census records, religious records, immigration and naturalization forms, etc.). The file's size will depend on your research style, how much information you uncover, and how much you choose to put in the binder.

Chapter 4

Genealogy by Computer

Computers can be very helpful to the genealogist in two ways:

- for data storage (software programs that help to organize and store information)
- To gather information and do research.

Since software programs are updated frequently and website addresses change often, the best strategy is to consult resources that can give you current information. Computer articles in genealogy journals, recent books, or *Genealogical Computing* magazine (see Appendix B) are important resources. For example, *Genealogical Computing* annually publishes a list of computerized genealogical databases. Many historical and genealogical societies have computer interest groups which can provide information and strategies to suit your needs. Some community colleges offer courses in genealogy by computer.

Software Programs

There are a number of genealogical computer software programs that will make your record-keeping task easier. *It is important to remember that computer software does not replace keeping paper files*; you will still want documentation for your information. And, while computers can speed up the task of compiling information, it is especially important to take care when entering the information: be meticulous about spelling and dates.

Genealogy software programs use the standard charts to record the data you have gathered. The advantage of these programs is that they can combine data in useful ways and keep it accessible; they are also very easy to update. Computers can sort information in various ways and index your files.

The programs differ in the way data is entered, how much space is available for data, layout and design of charts and reports, and word processing functions. Explore a few options to see which format you prefer before settling on one program. Many systems have a demo (demonstration) version on various servers or at a web site, which is a great way to try them out. Software programs are updated often, so try current versions when you are in the market to buy one.

Some of the more popular programs are reviewed here. Their addresses are provided on page 23–24.

Personal Ancestral File

This is the most popular program and among the most inexpensive. It is easy to learn and use, so it's a good choice if you're a beginner. The program is flexible, allowing you to adapt certain functions to your needs. It was developed by the Church of Jesus Christ of Latter-day Saints and is connected to their GEDCOM utility, which enables you to send and receive data to and from different software programs. (The Church has a huge data base of pedigrees on CD-ROM called Ancestral File; if you find a line of your own in those files, GEDCOM enables you to copy the pedigree and insert it into your own ancestry chart. Be sure to verify all information from copied pedigrees, however, since their accuracy is not verified.)

Family Tree Maker

This program is also easy to use and has the special benefit of producing professional charts in a range of formats. It doesn't have the power or flexibility of some other programs (for example, with the sorting function), but it is a good choice if your main purpose is to produce high-quality ancestry charts easily and artistically.

Everyone's Family Tree

An easy-to-learn program, this program (for IBM-compatible computers) provides features for more extensive genealogical projects. It is based on the "Dollarhide System" of genealogy. This effective organizational system uses shortcuts to accomplish functions and contains a Research Log. There is a help screen for each step of the program.

Roots

CommSoft has been evolving this program for a while; each updated version incorporates improvements over earlier versions. This IBM-compatible program may take longer to learn but it has many features and more flexibility than other programs. In addition to its own technical support, Roots user groups and books are available to help you become familiar with the Roots program. (The most popular is from the Computer Genealogy Society of San Diego, P.O. Box 370357, San Diego, CA 92137).

Computer Research

Computers allow you to access more information faster and easier than ever before. Many records are now available on CD-ROM through genealogy publishers (see Appendix A). Be careful though. Much of this information has been electronically scanned or reentered from original and compiled sources, so the chance of error is relatively high. The wisest strategy is to find what you need by computer, then consult the original document for verification.

The Internet provides access to numerous chat groups and a wealth of information on the worldwide web. You can often get research hints or solve genealogical problems through discussions with other genealogists. Since addresses change frequently, it is best to browse, using keywords to narrow your search as much as possible. One very useful resource is the ability to access many library databases (card catalogs) through Telnet; you can find out what books are available on a given topic, and which libraries have them.

The Church of Jesus Christ of Latter-day Saints offers Ancestral File (a database of genealogies of more than six million individuals), the International Genealogical Index, and its library catalog at its Family History Libraries. Searching the Ancestral File is easy but be aware that the accuracy of the genealogies, which have been submitted by many sources, has not been verified. The IGI is a list of the names and events in records held by the church and submitted by others. These records are available on CD-ROM at most family history centers (call 1-800-346-6044 for the library closest to you).

Many genealogical publishers sell genealogical files containing public records or indexed files on CD-ROM. Contact the organization directly for a catalog and price list (see Appendix). Most of these publishers are accessible on the worldwide web and may offer other services that can help you.

A few addresses of interest:

> The Library of Congress:
> http://lcweb.loc.gov/homepage/lchp.html

> The National Archives:
> http://www.nara.gov

> National Genealogical Society:
> http://www.genealogy.org/~ngs

> New England Historical Genealogical Society:
> http://www.nehgs.org

Computer Software Program Addresses

Everyone's Family Tree:

Dollarhide Systems, Inc.
203 Holly Street
Bellingham, WA 98225
(206) 671-3808
1-800-733-3807

Family Roots:

Quinsept, Inc.
P.O. Box 216
Lexington, Massachusetts 02173
(617) 641-2930

Family Tree Maker:

Broderbund Software
PO Box 6125
Novato, CA 94948-6125
1-800-315-0669
http://www.familytreemaker.com

Personal Ancestral File:

Salt Lake Distribution Center
1999 West 1700 South
Salt Lake City, UT 84104-4233
800-537-5950
(801) 531-2584

Reunion:

Leister Productions, Inc.
P.O. Box 289
Mechanicsburg, PA 17055
(717) 697-1378
www.LeisterPro.com

Roots V:

CommSoft, Inc.
7795 Bell Road
P.O. Box 310
Windsor, CA 95492-0310
E-mail: info@cmmsft.com
(800) 327-6687 (information, sales)
(707) 838-4300 (general business)

Important Genealogical Practices to Know

Chapter 5

Naming Practices

As you gather information, you may notice patterns in family names. Your family, for example, may have its own favorite first names that keep cropping up. An older relative may know the reasons for this so be sure to ask. Some naming practices, however, were common to the general population at the time so it will be helpful for you to be aware of them.

Given names

Since infant death was much more common a few generations ago, some traditions that may seem odd to us now were fairly standard then. For example, if an infant died, the next child of that gender was often given the same name. As a result, when researching you may find that two siblings (or even more) had the same name. This can help you figure out birth order and approximate dates, if they are not indicated. For example, you can infer that the first child named, say, Jane, died between the birth of younger sisters with different given names and the birth of the second child named Jane.

Naming practices also usually followed cultural traditions, so that what was common in the country of origin was carried over to descendants. Among New England settlers, for example, first names were often of English or Hebrew (Biblical) origin or carried some moral significance. In many cultures it was (and still is) common to give the oldest son and daughter their parents' first names. Another common practice was to use surnames as first names, especially among boys, so that a son would carry his mother's maiden name.

If your ancestors were European, you should know that a common practice was to name the oldest son after his paternal grandfather, the second son for his maternal grandfather, and the third son for his father. Similarly, the oldest daughter was often named for her maternal grandmother, the second daughter for her paternal grandmother, and the third daughter after her mother.

Surnames

Surnames can reveal information, not only about the country of origin, but also about social class, occupation, locality, or parentage. Knowing the meaning of a surname can reveal a lot about your ancestors' lives before immigration, often revealing their background or interests. The origins of surnames fall into four main classifications:

- patronymic, inherited from the father

- topnonymic, derived from the name of a place or a physical or geographic feature (These may contain clues to help you locate a town of origin in another country)

- occupational surnames

- surnames based on nicknames

Patronymic names, those derived from the father's name, are very common in most cultures. The following prefixes or suffixes are variations of "son of":

son - English	Ibn - Arabic
sen - Danish	sohn/zohn - German
de - French	poulos - Greek
Tse - Chinese	ben - Hebrew

Mac - Irish	ovich, na - Russian
O' (grandson) - Irish	es, ez - Spanish
Fitz - Norman	ap, s - Welsh
wicz - Polish	

The most common problem faced by people tracing their immigrant ancestors is that, upon arrival, many of their names changed spelling, lost prefixes, suffixes, or were (often loosely) translated into English. Members of the same family, because they met different immigration officers upon arrival, often wound up with different spellings of their name. Officers, overworked and unfamiliar with foreign languages, tended to spell names phonetically (how it sounded). Immigrants did not usually know more than a few words of English, and rarely knew how to spell their name in English. Many did not have a surname when they arrived. It was common in the late 1800's for an immigrant to go by two different names at the same time, one in the native language and one in English. In addition, many immigrants chose to "Americanize" their names, often a generation or two after arrival.

In all such cases, your care in transcribing names exactly will help you identify when the names changed or when tracing the reasons for a change. The Soundex Code (see below) can be helpful in identifying alternate spellings for your surname, and possibly discovering ancestors in the process.

The Soundex System

The Soundex System, a Federal Works Project, was developed in the 1930's to systematize variations of the same name. It is an invaluable tool for finding branches of your family that may have been missing simply because their surname was spelled differently. It is a phonetic system which encodes last names so they match other similarly pronounced surnames. Since the 1880 census, all federal censuses have been indexed using the Soundex System, which allows you to search for relatives who may have had a different surname spelling.

To use the Soundex code, you must translate the surname into one letter followed by three numbers. To do this, begin by writing the full last name. Circle the first letter. This becomes the first digit of the Soundex code. Then cross out all vowels (A, E, I, O, U), the consonants Y, W, H and the second of any two consecutive letters that are the same. (For example: Cullen becomes CLN).

Now convert the remaining consonants to numbers as follows:

> B P F V and Q become 1
> C S K G J X Z 2
> D T 3
> L 4
> M N 5
> R 6

If two consecutive consonants have the same number (example, KS) convert them to one digit rather than duplicate the number (Cullen is now C45). Write "O" to fill out the required number of digits (4) if the name you're coding has too few (Cullen now becomes C450). Disregard any remaining letters in excess of four (remember that the first letter of the surname, vowel or consonant, is *always* the first digit of the Soundex code name). The Soundex code can now be used to search census records (see Chapter Ten).

Chapter 6

Answers to Commonly Asked Genealogical Questions

When tracing your family history, you might encounter some areas of potential confusion, e.g., how to chart an adoption, calculate approximate dates or handle multiple marriages. The following section answers the most commonly asked questions so you will be prepared in the event they apply to your project.

Adoption

Adopted family members should be treated genealogically as you would any other ancestor. If information is known about the birth parents, you may want to note it, but the individual should always be placed in the family with whom he or she was raised.

An adoption in your family tree can be hard to trace, but several organizations may be of help:

American Adoption Congress
1000 Connecticut Avenue, NW, Suite 9
Washington, DC 20036
(202) 483-3399

National Adoption Clearinghouse
10530 Rosehaven Street, Suite 400
Fairfax, VA 22030
(703) 246-9095

Approximating Dates

You may be unable to find out dates of birth, marriage, or other events in an ancestor's life. In these cases, you may want to approximate a date rather than leave it blank. Always identify an approximated date as such, either with a "c." (circa) or "about," or parentheses around the date. Use as many clues as you can, such as children's birth dates. The following guidelines are statistical averages that may help approximate dates. Remember, though, that these patterns were more standard in past generations than in recent years.

> Average marriage age: man, 25; woman, 21
> Average age of parents at birth of first child: father, 26; mother, 22
> Average age of parents at birth of middle child: father, 32; mother, 28

Boundary Changes

Since your ancestors' time, boundaries of villages, counties, even countries may have changed and finding their birthplace or hometown can become difficult. Being aware that such changes occurred will save you frustration and time searching in the wrong place. When an older relative reminisces, try to get a description of the location as well as the place name. What was known locally in that place and time by a certain name may not appear on any maps or be familiar to residents today. Try to talk to older or longtime residents who may be familiar with a previous name or a "known as" name for a place.

Another solution is to contact your local historical society for help in locating maps of the region at the time your ancestors lived there.

Calendar Reform

Early American records sometimes contain a double date: for example, 21 January 1701/02. This confusion is a result of calendar reform. In trying to correct an earlier error, the day following 4 October 1582 was declared 15 October 1582. England did not accept this change until 1752, so that the day following 2 September 1752 was 14 September 1752. You might see double dating for the months January, February, or March in or before 1752 when New Year's Day, which had been March 25, was changed to January 1.

Multiple Marriages, Divorce

Multiple marriages have been common throughout history, in the past usually due to early deaths, more recently due to divorce. The genealogical practice is simply to label the first spouse with a (1) and the second, below the first, with a (2). Entering dates on the charts will help to clarify the marriages. If there were children by more than one spouse, you may choose to keep a separate family group sheet for each marriage for the sake of clarity, or enter all children on the same family sheet (the birth date order will clarify bloodlines). When there is a divorce, you can easily note that situation (entering a date may also be helpful).

In the case of an illegitimate birth, you may note that on your charts, but in all other ways treat the ancestor as you would anyone else on the chart. If one of the parents is not known, you can note that, but place the person in the family with whom she or he was raised or to whom he or she is related.

Relationship Terminology

In reading documents or letters, keep in mind that terms describing relationships did not always have the same meanings we use today. "Brother" or "sister," for example, signified a close relationship or religious identity as well as a sibling relationship. In the time of premature deaths, separation by immigration and long working hours, cousins, godchildren, even close friends were often raised by adults who were not their parents, but the children considered each other siblings. "Mother" and "father" were used to refer to older people in the community; "aunt," "uncle," and "cousin" are used even today to refer affectionately to close friends. Be aware of these practices while you do research; do not make assumptions about relationships unless you find proof.

Gathering Information

Chapter 7

Family Records

The best place to begin a genealogical search is close to home. There you are likely to find a wealth of information. Let your relatives know about your project, and ask them for copies of documents or photographs that may be helpful in compiling your family's genealogy.

If you have a family Bible, especially one that has been passed down for several generations, you already have a valuable genealogical resource. Before official records were kept, many families recorded marriages, births, and deaths in the family Bible so if you have access to your family's, begin with that. Since the information was generally entered at the time it occurred, names and dates tend to be reliable.

If the Bible is not yours, arrange to have it copied and return it promptly (and in the same condition you received it). Check the date the Bible was printed because events that occurred before that time were either copied or recalled, which increases the chance of error. If the handwriting and ink vary with each entry, you can surmise that information was entered when it occurred and is reliable. But if the handwriting and ink are the same for several entries, the information may have been entered at a later date from memory or transcribed from an earlier source, which is more prone to error. *As with any important research, you should verify all information in at least two sources.*

Other useful family items are mentioned below. Any of these can verify information or offer hints to investigate further.

- certificates and religious records (birth, death, baptism, confirmation and bar/bat mitzvah, marriage, death, funeral, cemetery)
- school records (roster/admissions, yearbooks, class photographs, report cards, awards, diplomas)
- letters, cards, postcards, invitations (wedding, baptism)
- diaries, journals
- scrapbooks, newspaper clippings
- passport/travel records
- immigration and naturalization records
- social security papers
- employment records
- club rosters
- military papers
- deeds and wills
- insurance papers
- health and medical records
- quilts, samplers (often include names, dates)
- engraved silverware, jewelry
- trophies
- inscriptions in books
- family recipes
- photographs

Be sure to copy all original documents and preserve the originals in your files (by ancestor's name or code number). See Chapter 12 for ways to preserve delicate original documents.

While these items provide factual information, learning the stories behind the names requires that you talk with family members. Chapter 13 and 14 discuss ways to gather stories and incorporate them into your family history.

If you decide to search for far-removed or lost relatives to broaden your research, don't overlook the option of advertising your search in newspapers or genealogical journals. The results can be very gratifying. Some family organizations publish newspapers with genealogical inquiries and answers. You can place an advertisement or letter in the *Genealogical Helper* or several other publications. Many genealogical journals contain space for such inquiries or family association names.

Chapter 8

Libraries and Other Research Resources

So much information can be found at or borrowed from (or through) your local public library that, after locating your family records, it is the logical place to continue your research. Before you go to the library, review the information you already have and narrow your focus to one individual or family, then narrow your search further to a birth or death date, for example. Bring your filled-in Ancestry Chart and family group sheets. Remember, too, that research librarians can be among the most valuable resources your library has to offer. Other resources include:

- a genealogical section. Many, but not all, libraries have them and many also work closely with a local historical society or genealogical library

- old maps

- census records which can be borrowed by your local library and read on their microfiche/film readers (see Chapter 10)

- city directories (which were often kept beginning in the late 1800's). These alphabetically list the name, address, occupation and employer of those living within the city limits. The addresses can be extremely helpful in verifying the identity of your ancestor in other records

- compiled records, including local and family histories and biographies. These are secondary sources and more apt to

41

contain errors than primary records. Their principal value is in providing an overview of the time or place in which your ancestor lived.

- newspapers are useful sources for verifying information, almost all have marriage and death notices. Microfilming and indexing newspapers has become common, so the information is more accessible than ever. The American Antiquarian Society (Worcester, Massachusetts) has indexed marriage and death notices in many national newspapers; this index is available at the New York Public Library, the Library of Congress, and through the New England Historic Genealogical Society.

- other indexes, many of which are available at local public libraries, such as Ayer's *Newspaper Guide*, Gregory's *List of American Newspapers 1821-1936* and Clarence S. Brigham's *History and Bibliography of American Newspapers, 1690-1820.*

- printed genealogies (though it's important to verify all information, since their accuracy varies). Their indexes can help you locate a certain name in family genealogies or local histories. Even if your family is not specifically mentioned, local histories in the town or county of your ancestor's residence can provide clues about where most residents were from originally.

The following sources provide extensive lists of published genealogies:

- Kaminkow, Marion J. *Genealogies in the Library of Congress: A Bibliography of Family Histories of America and Great Britain.*

- Long Island Historical Society. *Catalogue of American Genealogies in the Library.*

- New York Public Library. *Dictionary Catalog of the Local History and Genealogy Division, the Research Libraries of the New York Public Libraries.*

- Newberry Library, Chicago. *The Genealogical Index.*

- For families with New England roots, the New England Historical Genealogical Society has consolidated indexes to the genealogies printed in *The New England Historical and Genealogical Register* since 1847.

Other helpful resources are *Genealogical Books in Print* (edited by Netti Schreiner-Yantis) and the following national resources:

The Family History Library
35 North West Temple
Salt Lake City, UT 84150
(801) 240-2584
Call 800-346-6044 to find the library nearest you.

Library of Congress
1st Street & Independence Ave., SE
Washington, DC
(202) 707-5522

The National Archives
Pennsylvania Avenue at 8th Street, NW
Washington, DC 20408
(202) 501-5400
www.nara.gov

New York City Public Library
Local History and Genealogy Division
Fifth Avenue and 42nd Street
New York, NY 10018
(212) 930-0828
www.nypl.org/research/chss/lhg/genea.html

Newberry Library
60 West Walton Street
Chicago, IL 60610
(312) 943-9090

Remember that you can browse the catalogs of many libraries through Telnet.

Other research resources

Once you have familiarized yourself with the library's resources, it is also useful to check with local genealogical or
historical societies which are often staffed with interested,
knowledgeable volunteers. Being a member of a genealogical
group can be helpful, especially when you are faced with a
specific problem, and networking can be valuable in innu-
merable ways. You might find a society relevant to your ancestors' national background which can help with specific
problems. Large genealogical societies can provide information as well as resources. Many have lending libraries, sponsor lectures and conferences, and provide journals to members. Check the *Directory of Historical Societies and Agencies in the United States and Canada*, published by the American Association for State and Local History. Some genealogical groups are listed below:

The National Genealogical Society
4527 North 17th Street North
Arlington, VA 22207
(703) 525-0050
www.genealogy.org/~ngs

The New England Historic and Genealogical Society
101 Newbury Street
Boston, MA 02116
(617) 536-5740
www.nehgs.org

The Federation of Genealogical Societies
P.O. Box 3385
Salt Lake City, UT 84110

The Daughters of the American Revolution
1776 D Street, NW
Washington, DC 20006
e-mail: revolt@dar.com

Chapter 9

Public Records

Primary sources, those written at the time of the event (for example, birth and death certificates and naturalization papers), can be found in the National Archives (including 13 regional archives), state archives, county courthouses, and city and town halls. It is important to know what information is available from various agencies. For city, county, and state resources, consult *Ancestry's Red Book: American State, County and Town Sources* edited by Alice Eichholz.

Many vital records can be found in town, city, and state offices. For birth, death, and marriage records, contact the office of the city or town clerk who has jurisdiction over the area where the event occurred. There is usually a fee for certified copies by mail. You will need to know the person's full name, approximate date of the event, and the location of the event. Keep queries polite, simple, short, and always include a self-addressed, stamped envelope.

By 1920, all states required that birth and death records be kept and many began keeping them even earlier. The local Bureau of Vital Statistics maintains city and county birth and death records. State records are kept in a central registry, often in the state capitol. You can visit these offices in person, send a request by mail, or hire a professional genealogist or researcher (see Chapter 1) to conduct the search for you.

The office of the clerk of court often has a surname index. If not, each volume of records should contain an index to help you locate an individual's birth, marriage, or death records.

Marriage records

These records include licenses (applications) and certificates. Licenses are usually issued by the county clerk, while marriage records are usually filed with the county recorder. You can often search the registry lists and dockets on your own. The registry is a listing by marriage year and spouses' names (male surname, female maiden name), so, assuming you know the marriage year, it is easy to discover a wife's name if you know the husband's (or vice-versa).

The docket, which summarizes the marriage application (names of parties, addresses, date of application), can help you confirm information from the registry. This is where any other information you have, such as an address, can help you find the right information. Once you locate the correct docket, the serial number will lead you to the actual marriage certificate in the bureau's files. The marriage certificate contains additional information, including who performed the ceremony and where it took place.

Church Records

You can contact the pastor of the church your ancestors attended. Church records usually contain detailed, reliable information, including baptismal dates, birthplace and date, the names of one or both parents, and the names of a witness, guardian, or sponsor. Churches also keep burial records and membership lists. If the church no longer exists, contact the local church headquarters or historical society to find out where the records are kept.

Birth certificates contain:

- full name

- parentage and country of origin

- state and city of birth

- parents' names, ages, residences, and occupations

- the number of other children born to the mother, whether living or dead

- the attending physician's name

Death records provide:

- name

- name of informant*

- name of coroner

- burial place

- birth date and place

- cause of death

- names and birthplaces of parents

* Be aware that the accuracy of information in a death certificate depends on the relationship and state of mind of the informant.

Legal Records

Other civil records, specifically probate records, are also of interest to genealogists.

Land records can reveal information about when an individual entered a county and the county and state he or she lived in previously. If land was left to heirs, information on children (names, residences, daughters' husbands' names) can be found. Keep in mind that in frontier America, land was cheap and accessible so land records were not just for the well-to-do. It may be useful to know that in the east, boundaries were set by natural or artificial markers ("metes" and "bounds"), while the rest of the country used a rectangular survey system.

Probate records are where you will find individuals' last wills. (It may be useful to consult a reference for reading old wills, since their language can be difficult to interpret.) Wills were more common in rural and agrarian communities than in large cities. They are useful genealogical tools, often revealing relationships among individuals, information on previous residence, date of death, and the existence of other records. The executor is often a relative of the deceased person, so make note of his or her name.

Probate court records contain other legal documents, such as:

- petitions for probate of will
- guardianship papers
- adoption records
- delayed birth certificates
- name changes
- secret marriages
- land records
- notices to creditors
- affidavits
- letters of administration
- inventories and appraisements
- petitions to determine heirship

Depending on the state, probate records are kept in probate or surrogate's court, superior court, circuit courts, or with the register of wills. The Secretary of State's office in each state can provide you with information or a list of where to write to obtain probate court records.

Court files contain other records, such as depositions, records of lawsuits, and other court actions.

In searching for records, be sure to familiarize yourself with the history of the location for possible boundary changes to make sure that you look in the right place.

Military Records

The National Archives has military records from 1775 to the present. The earliest federal records are the payrolls of soldiers in the Continental Army during the Revolutionary War. Service records include company rolls, rosters, enlistments, discharge records, pension records, prisoner of war records, and burial records. The National Archives, historical societies, and major genealogical libraries have indexes of military records.

Military histories, available at local and special libraries, are a possible source of information about a particular regiment. Don't overlook other public sources, such as town monuments or plaques, soldiers' letters (in city and county archives), and local newspapers for additional information.

For members of the Armed Services who died overseas, contact the Secretary of Defense, Washington, DC 20301; Coast Guard members' records can be obtained by contacting Commandant, P.S., U.S. Coast Guard, Washington, DC 20593. Further assistance can be obtained from the Office of Overseas Services, U.S. Department of State, Washington, DC 20593.

Social Records

Private organizations (Elks, Knights of Columbus, Lions) often keep records for many years. These vary in value but some contain names of family members and detailed biographies of members which can reveal more personal information. College fraternities and university clubs also have files which may be of use to the genealogist. Colleges themselves keep records (rosters, yearbooks) which may be of interest.

Cemetery Records

Cemeteries also keep records which contain birth and death dates and often contain data on other relatives in the same plot. You can write to the superintendent of the cemetery for a list of all interments in the plot (include a self-addressed, stamped envelope).

If you know the approximate death date and place, but not which cemetery to search, the local historical society should be able to tell you which cemeteries were in use at that time. (Remember that the burial site is listed on the death certificate.) Again, since boundaries often changed, check with bordering towns, too. Knowing the religious denomination of your ancestor can help narrow your search to certain cemeteries.

Gravestone inscriptions can be good genealogical sources. They usually include the full name, birth date, and date of death. Old stones are more likely to have a message which may reveal personal information about the person or survivors. If you visit a cemetery, it is wise to take a photograph or rubbing (use a crayon or carpenter's pencil on butcher's paper) or to sketch the stone and copy the inscription exactly. Old stones may contain illegible or obsolete words. Note the exact location of the stone, and examine nearby stones (relatives were often buried near each other).

Chapter 10

Census Records

Federal census schedules are valuable resources for genealogists but they do have substantial drawbacks. The first is that, while the federal government has taken a census every 10 years since 1790, they are not generally available to the public (to protect living individuals' privacy) except for the years 1790 to 1920. Second, while they reveal vital information, they are filed geographically rather than alphabetically, so you must first know the residence, or at least the home county (or in cities, the ward), of the ancestor you are researching.

As previously noted in the section on the Soundex Code System, federal censuses have been indexed by Soundex Code since 1880. Because families often lived near each other, and census information is compiled as it is encountered geographically, it is worth checking listings before and after those you are searching, you may find other ancestors.

The National Archives has census schedules for the years 1790-1870, the 1880 census on microfilm, parts of the 1890 schedules (most was destroyed by fire), and the 1900 microfilmed census.

The National Archives and its branch centers have microfilm copies of the censuses for your use. You may borrow the microfilm rolls to read at your local library or the genealogical libraries of the Church of Jesus Christ of Latter-day Saints (check to be sure they have a microfilm reader, preferably one from which you can make copies). Ask your local librarian about ordering procedures; there may be a small charge. It is also possible to purchase the microfilm rolls from the National Archives.

While census records are excellent resources, another drawback is that they are incomplete (many are missing) and their accuracy depends, not only on the census-taker, but on the person giving the information. Since the accuracy of census information varies, you should consult three consecutive censuses to verify information.

Increasingly detailed information was collected with every census after 1850. The following table lists the information you can expect to find in each census year.

1790-1840:

name of head of household (oldest, or primary property holder)
all persons in household: age range and gender

1850-1870:

name of all persons in household:
gender
age
relationship to head of household
birthplace (territory, state, or country)
occupation

1880-1920:

for all persons in household, in addition to information from previous censuses:
description ("color")
marital status
notation if unemployed
illness or disability
parents' names and birthplaces

1920:
_____

in addition to information from previous censuses:
native language of parents
education
occupation
literacy

During some census years, in addition to the federal census, special censuses were conducted. Some examples follow:

- In southern states, the 1850 and 1860 schedules contain information on the age and gender of slaves under the owner's name.

- Mortality schedules, which reveal the name, age, sex, birthplace, occupation, month and cause of death for all household members who died in the preceding year, are available for 1850, 1860, 1870, and 1880.

- Agriculture schedules, containing information on land holdings and what crops were planted.

- Manufacturing schedules, which lists the items manufactured, number of employees, and annual income, were also occasionally conducted.

- In 1890, there was a Special Census of Union Civil War Veterans and their Widows, most of which is still available.

Under certain circumstances, you can obtain more current census information. Census information on a deceased person must be requested by the surviving spouse, immediate family, beneficiary, or executor of the estate. Send a copy of the death certificate with your request. There is a fee for searches conducted by the Census Bureau; contact them for information on fees and procedures.

Local Censuses

Many states and counties conducted censuses in non-federal-census years. These often contain more genealogical detail than the federal censuses. To find out what censuses (if any) were conducted in your ancestor's locality, check with a reference librarian or genealogical library.

Chapter 11

Immigrant, African American and Native American Ancestors

Immigrant Ancestors

From 1820 to 1930, 38 million immigrants arrived in the United States, and many of our ancestors were among them. Whatever their country of origin, if you have decided to delve into that portion of your family's history, the immigrant ancestor requires special search strategies and offers rich rewards.

Immigration Records

There are arrival records for immigrants, and several sources in your library can help you locate them. Try *They Came in Ships: A Guide to Finding Your Immigrant Ancestor's Arrival Record* by John Phillip Coletta (Salt Lake City: Ancestry, 1989).

The federal government required ship captains to keep passenger lists which are valuable to the genealogist. The lists can verify your ancestor's age, occupation, and arrival date. Records exist for Atlantic Coast (Baltimore, Boston, Mobile, New Bedford, New Orleans, New York, and Philadelphia) and Gulf of Mexico ports. Pacific Coast lists were destroyed by fire, but the California Historical Society (2099 Pacific Avenue, San Francisco, CA 94109) has lists and indexes prepared from other sources for persons arriving in California from 1820 to 1869.

Though the amount of detail varies, most lists contain:

- the name of the ship and captain
- the date and port of the ship's arrival
- the name of the port of embarkation
- the embarkation date
- each passenger's name, age, and occupation

There are indexes to most of the immigration passenger lists, but many are arranged chronologically, so it is helpful to know the name of the port of entry, the exact or approximate arrival date, and the name of the ship. You can find the ship's name from the records of vessel entrances at the ports (now at the National Archives), especially if you know the port the ship left from. These records contain the name of each vessel, the captain's name, and the date of arrival. You might want to consult a reference book such as *Morton Allan Directory of European Passenger Steamship Arrivals* to determine the name and arrival date of ship arriving in New York 1890-1930 and Philadelphia, Boston, and Baltimore, 1904-1926.

Customs Passenger Lists are kept at the National Archives. Early records not maintained by the Archives may be on file in the State Archives of the port of arrival. Indexes exist for most, but not all, passenger lists.

The National Archives has passenger lists of the following arrivals:

Baltimore from	1820-1919
Boston	1883-1899
New Orleans	1820-1897
New York City	1820-1919

Naturalization

Most immigrants went through the process of becoming citizens. If your ancestor did, naturalization records will give you more information. These records are usually kept by the clerk of court for the district which issued the naturalization certificate. You can sometimes discover the name of the court from the voter lists in the county where your ancestor resided; some county lists are in the National Archives. Since 1801, there has been a five-year waiting period for naturalization so the year of arrival is fairly easy to determine from the naturalization application. Records after September 16, 1906 are kept with the Immigration and Naturalization Service, Washington, DC 20536 (submit form N-585 from any district office of the Service). Since the petition contains a lot of family information, it is recommended that you request the entire petition (otherwise you will get just the first page). There is a basic fee for searches.

Naturalization records contain:

- name
- age
- physical description (height, skin color, complexion, eye/hair color, distinguishing marks)
- name of spouse
- residence
- names, ages, and residence of children
- country (or even hometown) of origin
- place (port) and date of entry (sometimes)

If you are tracing your European history, the following list of basic terms will help you locate places by their foreign names:

state or country	county	town or city
Denmark	amt	by or stad
England	shire, county	borough, city
Finland	laani	kyla, kauppala, kaupunki
France	departement	village, ville
Germany	kreis	ort, dorf, stadt
Iceland	sysla	sokn, baer
Ireland	shire	borough, city
Netherlands	provincie	dorp, stad
Norway	amt, fylker	by, sogn, stad
Scotland	shire	registration branch, city
Sweden	lan	by, koping, stad
Switzerland	bezirk, kanton	dorf, stadt
Wales	swydd	pentre, terf, dinas

If you know your ancestor's birthplace in Europe, you can write to the Bureau of Vital Statistics of the city or town for birth, marriage, or death data on an individual. Include as many facts as you can (full name, date and destination of emigration) in your request, and be sure to inquire about fees. The various embassies in Washington, DC, can also provide information on genealogical material. Some countries kept very careful records; you may be lucky and get a lot of information this way.

If you decide to gather data from Europe, consult a reference book on the availability of and strategies for gathering genealogical information from Europe. Many genealogical libraries have European records in their collections. You can check directly with them to see what resources are available.

African American Ancestry

If some or all of your ancestors were African American, you may encounter difficulties that require research strategies over and above those previously described.

A good first step is to contact a genealogical or historical society that specializes in African American genealogy*. If you search in the usual places, you might not find records where you would expect to because, until 1954, many towns, cities, and states kept African-American records separate from white records. Since, even now, many clerks might not be aware of this situation, be sure to request black as well as white records. It is also less likely that black records are indexed.

Even where compiled records exist, it is important to know that black records were often omitted. Therefore, if you do not find your ancestor listed, find and check the original records. One inventory that might prove helpful is the WPA Historical Records Survey conducted in the 1930's. This index lists vital records by county. The Freedmen's Bureau, established in 1865, kept careful records which are rich genealogical resources. These records, and detailed bank records from the Freedman's Savings and Trust Company, are housed in the National Archives.

When researching a slave ancestor, it is helpful to know the name of the slave's owner since all records would be filed under his name. In addition, use standard genealogical resources, such as military records and census records, which can be of great help.

While your search will probably require persistence and patience, as always, the rewards are worth any temporary frustration.

* Afro-American Historical Genealogical Society
   1407 14th Street, NW
   Washington, DC
   (202) 234-5350

Native American Ancestry

One unique aspect of Native American tradition is its matrilineal culture. If you are of Native American descent, your strategy will be to follow the woman's name back. If your ancestry is entirely American, you should probably simply use the ancestry chart substituting even numbers for women and odd numbers for their male spouses.

For information on events that occurred after 1824, tribal records can be obtained through the Bureau of Indian Affairs. Earlier records were filed with the BIA's predecessor, the War Department. These records go back to 1789. There are also many resource books pertaining to Native American ancestry that are worth consulting (see Recommended Reading).

The oldest and most accurate records will probably be found within the tribe. The tribal council can best direct your efforts here.

Sharing Your Family History

Chapter 12

Preserving Family Treasures

The preservation of old photographs, original documents, letters, recipes, and other valued papers requires special care. In general, use the suggested guidelines for photographs to preserve any valuable, original documents.

Perhaps the most treasured of all genealogical possessions are old photographs which evoke memories and imagination in unique ways. Original photographs are certainly worth careful preservation, since there is only one and in many cases there is no negative. The original may be tinted or airbrushed, so that even if a negative or quality copies are made, the original remains unique.

There are three main areas of concern about photographs:

- restoring and preserving originals
- reproducing originals (including negatives, enlarging, cropping)
- displaying photographs (in an album or frame)

The principal enemies of photographs are acid, heat, humidity, and sunlight. If the photographs you have are not safe — for example, stored in a damp place, or crumbling in boxes — the first thing to do is remove them from these conditions. If they appear to be in good condition but their album or frame smells musty, it is wise to take the photographs out, since decay can occur even though they are in a "safe" place.

If the photographs are in an album, examine it carefully. PVC plastic causes damage to photos and the adhesives and covers of newer magnetic albums also cause deterioration to photographs. Older albums, those with plain paper, the photographs mounted with adhesive corners, are relatively safe. Although the need is not so urgent, you may decide to remount these photos in a better-quality album with sturdier pages. Always wear cotton gloves when handling photographs to avoid oils smudging the image.

When remounting photographs, look for archival materials. Many photography and art supply stores carry these, as do the suppliers listed at the end of this chapter. Use albums with acid-free paper or polypropylene or polyester (Mylar brand) plastic. For original documents, remove staples and clips, and store them flat (unfold gently). Protective plastic sleeves will preserve them (never laminate originals, as this causes deterioration).

Be sure to identify the photographs as you rearrange them; even if you don't know much, write whatever you can figure out. Notes written on post-it notes and attached to the back of photographs are effective, since no pressure is placed on the photograph itself. Once the photographs are carefully in place, you can transfer information to album pages.

Don't be discouraged by a large box of unidentified photographs. While it may be too late to identify each one, you can discover an amazing amount of material using a few process-of-elimination skills.

You probably have old photographs in all shapes and sizes. This will prove very helpful in your detective work. First, match up photographs by size and border style: old photographs generally have straight edges or serrated ones. Look at the backs of photographs: aside from handwritten notes, you may find a printed number. Each photograph from one roll of film was marked with the same number, so if you have information on one photograph, you now have it for all pictures from that roll. You may have only a couple of photographs with information (a name or date written on the back), but by matching others from the same roll of film, you may recognize the same subjects and can certainly infer that the date (or at least the year) is the same.

Once you have grouped photographs in this way and identified what you can, run them past relatives. Even if you do not have one relative who knows everything, try to get a few family members together, they will often jar each other's memory to arrive at a date or name.

If you have an older relative who can provide stories to go with the photographs, you are very fortunate. Sometimes family members, usually reluctant to talk about the past, will become talkative when faced with a photograph and an interested listener. You may find that "interviewing" a family member about photographs is more effective than a general interview (see Chapter 13), especially if you are not sure what to ask or if the person's health is failing (it is very easy to do this kind of talking in short sessions). You will probably find it easiest to label the photographs (with numbers on post-it notes) and to write notes on separate paper with corresponding numbers, then organize the information later.

Restoring and Preserving

There are many more options for restoring and preserving photographs than there used to be, but it is still important to be careful, especially in your choice of a photography shop. If you are getting an original restored or getting a negative or copies made from an original, it is best to avoid one-hour and chain stores, whose specialty is speed and bulk (and, often, price). Find a reputable photographic shop that does its own developing and has experience with old and delicate photographs; these are your irreplaceable photographs and you cannot be too careful about finding the service you deserve. It is tragic yet all too common in our fast-paced world for shops to mistreat original photographs or lose negatives. You might get your money back, but there's no recovering the image. *Ask the proprietor if he or she does the developing in-house.* Even if he or she does, you **must** request that it be done in-house *each time you bring work.* If you don't, your negative could be mailed away and, unfortunately, anything can happen then.

If an original photograph is damaged, there are several options. One (the only one available until recently) is to painstakingly restore the original photograph. This is expensive and requires great skill. If it is a treasured photograph and you have a photographer you trust, it may well be worth doing. Computerized duplication presents another option: to reproduce the original, then touch up the reproduction. This is quite inexpensive and can be done quickly. This is generally the best option for snapshots but you may want to make the investment in professional work for portraits. The computerized method can also make such changes as adjusting the light/contrast (more or less light), removing distracting background objects (or even people), and cropping to achieve a more professional image easily, quickly, and at low cost. See the bibliography for more information.

Copying

A little-known fact about copies or enlargements is that in standard photographic practice, the size requested is the size of the paper, not the actual image. So, while a 5" x 7" photograph is printed on 5" x 7" paper, the image is slightly smaller, with a white border. If you want the image to be 5" x 7" (to avoid a white border showing in a 5" x 7" frame, for example), tell the proprietor this; the photograph can be developed on larger paper, usually for the same price. In printing photographs, there are lots of options, and the customer can be as involved as he or she wants to be. If you do not make any special requests, the proprietor will make certain decisions (which may be fine with you). But if you want something done in a certain way (even if you think it's obvious), say so: you have every right to get what you want.

For example, some old portraits are artistic, with a balanced focus, e.g., between a bride's face and flowers. In reprinting such a photograph, the proprietor may assume you want the subject's face centered, and will crop what he or she considers excess. If you want the composition of the image to remain the same, you **must** be clear about this. If the proprietor balks at your requests, go elsewhere: these are treasured possessions and should be handled by someone who respects them.

Displaying

Now that you have quality photographs that you're proud of, you'll want to display them appropriately. In addition to aesthetics, be sure to make choices that preserve them. There are many archival materials available today that are sensitive to delicate photographs. Archival materials are also available for framing photographs. While the value of such materials is debatable, the difference in price is so small that it may be worth it in peace of mind. Using traditional mounting corners to display photographs gives a classic look to the album and places little stress on the photographs. If you have photos mounted this way, breathe easy, you may choose to remount them on archival paper but you can be confident that the photos are in good condition. Mounting corners make an excellent choice for old photographs, not only because they are gentle, but aesthetically they suit the time period of older photos. A nice touch is to write (use pens made especially for this) on the album pages to identify the photos. You might want to arrange the album like a scrapbook, including written memories, stories, recipes, and other mementos. The catalogs of archival materials provided by the companies below will give you plenty of ideas.

The Archival Company
P.O. Box 1239
Northampton, MA 01061-1239
800-442-7576
http://www.archivalco.com

AGLL Genealogical Services
P.O. Box 329
593 West 100 North
Bountiful, Utah 84011-0329
800-658-7755
801-298-5468 (fax)
e-mail: sales@agll.com

Chapter 13

Gathering Family Stories

Now that you have done the research and gathered factual information about your ancestors, you have completed your *genealogy*. Your real *family history*, however, is made up of much more than names and dates; it is stories, traditions, religion, recipes, all the elements of individual lives. Family records are important because the real fabric of people's lives are found in their letters, diaries, hobbies, and evidence of other interests.

Talking to older members of your family is an important way to gain insight into the way your ancestors lived and bring the facts you've gathered to life. The individual information sheet is a sketch of personal information. Your family is a tremendous resource for gathering details and making your ancestors' lives more vivid.

Interviewing Relatives

It is never too late to gather family stories (and if you think there are none, you're wrong). You will discover many funny, fascinating tales from the past when you encourage people to recall and relate them. Interviewing relatives will reveal and "humanize" details of your ancestors' lives. If you choose to write a family history, these stories are what will "bring them to life" once more.

Relatives can be interviewed individually or in a group, in a simple conversational exchange or by audio or videotape. How you choose to conduct the interview(s) is determined by practicality and preferences. A one-on-one interview is very different from a discussion in which several people's memories interact. Interviewing several family members together is usually a more casual interview and can yield vivid, entertaining stories as relatives jar each other's memories. Here, your role as interviewer will be more hands-off; one general question can keep a few people busy for several minutes.

Before the Interview

Whether you interview in person or by telephone, make an appointment well ahead of time. This is not only courteous but gives the person to be interviewed time to recall memories. Give your subject a general idea about the nature of your questions and, if you'd like, ask him or her to gather items that may be of interest. This is the perfect way to open a discussion of family heirlooms and to learn the "stories" behind them. Consider reviewing a list of questions with the subject ahead of time. Pick the questions together, this ensures that the person to be interviewed is interested in the subjects selected and ready to talk about them. Remember, the more preparation, the more successful the interview will be.

During the Interview

No matter what format you use, your role during the interview is to direct the discussion to areas of interest or importance, to listen, and to spur the talk on when necessary. Don't be impatient when people wander off the subject a little. If they're relaxed and following their own memories, a lot can be revealed. Questioning is a skill, and the value of the interview depends very much on the questions you ask.

Try to keep questions simple, direct, and unbiased, and avoid yes/no questions as much as possible. Take notes during the interview, especially of names and dates, even if it is recorded. Try to arrange for a follow-up interview, especially if time is short or you are interviewing several relatives at once. A second meeting will allow you to gather information you may have missed in the first interview, or to confirm information you're not sure of.

Tips for a Successful Interview

- Limit the session to 1 - 1½ hour.

- Be sure you and your subject(s) are comfortable.

- Limit distractions.

- If audio or videotaping, begin by introducing the subject and yourself, the date and place (if taking notes in writing, be sure to include this information).

- Start with general, factual questions to get the subject comfortable.

- Listen and respond when appropriate; encourage your subject, gently guide the conversation only if it strays.

- Let the interviewee be aware of your interest in the subject; listen intently, maintain eye contact.

- Ask questions on a range of topics: childhood and family memories, school, career, marriage, and children.

- Include some questions that are general or philosophical ("Do you have any thoughts on marriage you would like to share?").

- Ask open-ended questions (not factual, yes/no questions).

- Take breaks whenever appropriate (especially for older family members, be aware of energy levels).

- Be tactful when addressing touchy issues (there almost always are some).

- Let the subject's responses lead to other questions: if an answer isn't clear, ask him/her to elaborate; if a response makes you think of another question, ask it.

- After the interview, if this is not a close relative, make sure your subject knows how to get in touch with you in case he or she would like to add anything.

In general, try to go beyond "ordinary" questions, so the subject will be encouraged to share the essence of himself/herself or the person she or he is talking about. Consider questions on nicknames, occupational history, education (favorite subject, books), talents (artistic? humorous? athletic?), family traditions, hobbies, favorite foods, interesting habits. For example: What was she or he like? Are there any characteristics that stand out? What were his or her habits? hobbies? What did she or he do for fun? You can get some good interview questions from books and articles (see Croom and Huberman in Recommended Reading).

Correspondence

If it isn't practical to interview a relative in person or by telephone, the next best approach is to get the desired information in writing. It is important not to overwhelm the recipient: if you ask for too much or are vague you risk getting no response at all. If the person is receptive, you can always follow up with more questions later.

Make your request clear and direct. Let the person know why you are seeking this information, then write specific questions you would like answered, leaving room for responses right on the letter. Anything you do to make the job easier for the recipient is courteous and improves the chances of a response. Be sure to thank the person and enclose a self-addressed stamped envelope for their reply.

Chapter 14

Sharing Your Family History

There are several ways to share the family history you have now so carefully researched. You can write it, compile documents about it, or record the history with a tape recorder or VCR.

Writing a Family History

A written family history traditionally proceeds chronologically from past to present, each chapter containing the biography of an ancestor. It is usually written in narrative form and is based on the facts and stories you have gathered.

Computers make the process of writing such a history achievable for more people. Software programs help you organize and write your family history, and printing it out on a printer is easier, cheaper and faster than it used to be. Still, writing can be a daunting task for many of us. Here are some tips to help you:

- Read a few family histories before you begin (check with your local library or historical society).

- Organize your project into a manageable size; start small and invite relatives to help.

- Follow one line of the family.

- Imagine an audience as you write. Having a real person or persons in mind will help you establish a comfortable, conversational tone.

- Focus on the facts; let them guide the writing.

- Use the individual information sheets to guide the narrative.

- Write about one individual at a time, adding the spouse and children as you go.

- Quote from letters, diaries, newspaper articles.

- Include the ancestral chart and family information sheets as you discuss individuals.

- To enliven the narrative, add photographs, maps, copies of relevant documents and historical information if you wish.

In Book III of her published journal, Madeleine L'Engle reflects on her family's stories as she faces her mother's death. Here is an elegant example of a written family history, in which genealogical facts, the words of the subject's daughter, and the writer's memory are intertwined.

Mado was left penniless at the beginning of the war, with three small children, and everything else taken away from her. For a while she was the matron of a military hospital at Lake City, Florida, and, typically, nursed Northern and Southern soldiers with equal tenderness, for in her heart there was no North nor South. "Many Northern boys died in her arms," Mother told me. "One mother and father of a Yankee soldier were so grateful for her care of their son that they sent her a ring with a beautiful black pearl. It burned up in the great fire with so many other of our treasures.

Illness and death were daily companions in her life. She never ceased to grieve for her husband, but it was a quiet, personal grief; what she offered others was lov-

ing care and laughter. She wore only black and white for the rest of her life, though she did not carry an aura of mourning with her, but one of complete zest for life. She could have married many times over, but William the golden lad was the love of her life, and when she lay dying at the age of eighty-seven, she kept calling his name. She also asked for a dish of ice cream, which she ate with great appreciation and pleasure, and died shortly thereafter. Living or dying, I don't think Mado feared the heat of the sun.

— from Madeleine L'Engle's journal, *The Summer of the Great-Grandmother*, The Crosswicks Journal, Book Two (1974 HarperSanFrancisco): Book III, pp. 173)

Compiling Documents into a Family History

If writing doesn't appeal or seem appropriate to you, there are simpler ways to preserve the information you've gathered. You can compile interesting documents and photographs, then label and copy them for family members. Each set is an invaluable gift, one you can be sure will be treasured and revisited often.

Recording Your Family History

Another idea, growing in popularity, is to record your family history with a tape recorder or VCR. This can be as simple as a taped interview with a grandparent, or as elaborate as a professionally arranged compilation of photographs, maps, interviews, narrative, and "movie-type" music.

A few tips for do-it-yourself videotaping:

- choose a well-lit area (natural light and lamp light are more flattering than overhead lighting)

- use a tripod for stability

- use a separate microphone rather than the built-in one (they are too far from your subject and can sound hollow)

- if possible, have someone else control the camera so that you can focus on the interview

- to prevent accidental erasure, remove the Erase Tab from the videotape after taping

To personalize your presentation, you might want to dedicate it to someone, perhaps the oldest or youngest member of your family. Include a list of family names and addresses and distribute it to one and all. The more copies you make, the cheaper the per-copy cost will be and, if cost is an issue, some family members will probably be glad to contribute. For your information, many local libraries, genealogical libraries, and historical societies would also welcome a copy of your family history for their collections.

Now that you have compiled your family history, enjoy your accomplishment. If the project left you with new ideas about finding and sharing your ancestor's stories, we hope you will explore them. As a suggestion, a family tree makes a unique baby gift. Or, you might decide to plan a family reunion — it's the perfect way to gather more anecdotes, take photographs or videotape relatives.

Remember, your family history continues as long as your family lives and grows and has stories to tell.

Appendix A

Genealogical Publishers

AGLL Genealogical
Services

P.O. Box 329
Bountiful, UT 84011-0329
1-800-760-AGLL
e-mail: sales@agll.com

Deseret Book Direct

P.O. Box 30178
Salt Lake City, UT 84130-0178
1-800-453-4532
http://www.deseretbook.com

The Everton
Publishers, Inc.

P.O. Box 368
Logan, UT 84323-0368
1-800-443-6325
http://www.everton.com

Frontier Press

P.O. Box 3715, Dept. 1096
Galveston, TX 77552
(409) 740-7988
1-800-772-7559 (orders only)
e-mail: kgfrontier@aol.com
http://www.doit.com/frontier

Genealogy Unlimited, Inc.

P.O. Box 537
Orem, UT 84059-0537
1-800-666-4363
e-mail: genun@itsnet.com
http://www.itsnet.com/~genun

Appendix B

Genealogy Journals

Ancestry and *Genealogical Computing*
Ancestry
Dept. TG, P.O. Box 476
Salt Lake City, UT 84110-9859
1-800-ANCESTRY (262-3787)

Everton's Genealogical Helper
Everton Publishers
P.O. Box 368
Logan, UT 84321
1-800-443-6325

Heritage Quest and *Genealogy Bulletin*
Heritage Quest Subscription Dept.
P.O. Box 329
Bountiful, UT 84011-0329
1-800-658-7755
e-mail: sales@agll.com

National Genealogical Society Quarterly
National Genealogical Society
4527 17th Street, North
Arlington, VA 22207-2399
(703) 525-0050

Recommended Reading

African American Genealogical Sourcebook. Detroit: Gale Research, 1995.

An Ounce of Preservation: A Guide to the Care of Papers and Photographs. Tuttle, Craig. Highland City, Florida: Rainbow Books, 1995.

Asian American Genealogical Sourcebook. Detroit: Gale Research, 1995.

Computer Genealogy: A Guide to Research through High Technology. Pence, Richard A., ed. Salt Lake City: Ancestry, 1991.

Finding Our Fathers: A Guidebook to Jewish Genealogy. New York, 1997.

Hispanic American Genealogical Sourcebook. Detroit: Gale Research, 1995.

How to Find Your Family Roots. Beard, Timothy Field, with Denise Demong. New York: McGraw-Hill, 1977.

How to Trace Your Family Tree. Garden City: Doubleday, 1975. American Genealogical Research Institute Staff.

Native American Genealogical Sourcebook. Detroit: Gale Research, 1995.

Searching for Your Ancestors: the How and Why of Genealogy. Doane, Gilbert H. and James B. Bell. 5th ed. Minneapolis: University of Minnesota, 1980.

The Researcher's Guide to American Genealogy. Greenwood, Val D. Baltimore: Genealogical Publishing, 1978.

Tracing Your Roots. Editors of Consumer Guide. New York: Bell Publishing, 1977.

Unpuzzling Your Past: A Basic Guide to Genealogy. Croom, Emily Anne. 2nd ed. Cincinnati: Bettering Books, 1989.

Video Family Portraits. Huberman, Ron and Laura Janis. Bowie, MD: Heritage Books, 1987.

Voices in Your Blood: Discovering Identity through Family History. Vandagriff, G.G. Kansas City: Andrews & McMeel, 1993.

Index

A
adoption 31, 50
African American 57, 60, 61, 83
Ancestral File 20, 22, 23
Ancestry Chart 5, 7, 8, 14, 16, 17, 20, 21, 41, 62

B
Bible 37
birth records 17, 47, 48

C
cemetery records 38, 52
census 17, 29, 30, 41, 53, 54, 55, 56, 61
church records 22, 48
computers 19, 20, 21, 75

D
Daughters of the American Revolution 45
death records 17, 38, 47, 48, 49
directories 41
divorce 33

F
Family History Library 43
Family Information Sheet 5, 8, 10, 11, 14, 16, 17, 76

G
genealogical societies 19, 44, 45
genealogies 22, 42, 43
genealogists, professional 4

I
IGI (International Genealogical Index) 22
immigration records 17, 38, 57